1ST GRADE GEOGRAPHY: CONTINENTS OF THE WORLD

SPEEDY
PUBLISHING

Speedy Publishing LLC
40 E. Main St. #1156
Newark, DE 19711
www.speedypublishing.com

A continent is one of several very large landmasses on Earth. The 7 continents of the world are North America, South America, Antarctica, Europe, Asia, Africa and Australia.

ASIA

is the Earth's largest and most populous continent. Asia also contains the world's most populous country, China, and the world's largest country, Russia.

Mount Everest is the highest mountain on the Asian continent and the highest mountain in the world.

EUROPE

is the world's second-smallest continent by surface area. Most of Europe now uses the same currency called the Euro. Europe is home to the smallest country in the world, the Vatican.

The Eiffel Tower is located in Paris, France, on the continent of Europe.

AFRICA

is the world's second-largest and second-most-populous continent. Africa is one of the most diverse places on the planet with a wide variety of terrain, wildlife, and climates.

The Great Pyramid of Giza are located in the Giza, Egypt, on the continent of Africa.

AUSTRALIA

Australia is the smallest continent by size and the second smallest in terms of population. The name Australia means "land of the south".

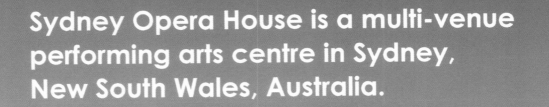

Sydney Opera House is a multi-venue performing arts centre in Sydney, New South Wales, Australia.

NORTH AMERICA

North America is the third largest of the seven continents. North America is a continent wholly within the Northern Hemisphere.

Niagara Falls is one of the oldest tourist attractions in North America.

SOUTH AMERICA

is the fourth largest continent in size and the fifth largest in population. The geography of western South America is dominated by the Andes mountains.

Angel Falls is the world's highest uninterrupted waterfall. These unique geological formations are found mostly in the Venezuelan Guiana Highland in South America.

ANTARCTICA

is Earth's southernmost continent, containing the geographic South Pole. About 98% of Antarctica is covered by ice.

Mount Erebus is the second highest volcano in Antarctica. It is the 6th highest ultra mountain on an island.

Made in the USA
Lexington, KY
23 February 2016